Off Of

Selected by New York theatre critics, professionals, and the editorial staff of Samuel French, Inc. as the most important plays of the Twenty-Eighth Off Off Broadway Original Short Play Festival sponsored by Love Creek Productions.

LEAVING TANGIER
by David Johnston

BLUEBERRY WALTZ
by Liz Amberly

ALONG FOR THE RIDE
by Jay D. Hanagan

A LOW-LYING FOG
by John Yearley

QUICK & DIRTY
(A Subway Fantasy)
by David Riedy

THE FERRY
by Ryan Hill

A SAMUEL FRENCH ACTING EDITION

SAMUEL FRENCH
FOUNDED 1830

SAMUELFRENCH.COM

ISBN   978-0-573-62960-0   Printed in U.S.A.   #17707

MUSIC USE NOTE

Licensees are solely responsible for obtaining formal written permission from copyright owners to use copyrighted music in the performance of this play and are strongly cautioned to do so. If no such permission is obtained by the licensee, then the licensee must use only original music that the licensee owns and controls. Licensees are solely responsible and liable for all music clearances and shall indemnify the copyright owners of the play and their licensing agent, Samuel French, Inc., against any costs, expenses, losses and liabilities arising from the use of music by licensees.

IMPORTANT BILLING AND CREDIT REQUIREMENTS

All producers of *LEAVING TANGIER, BLUEBERRY WALTZ, ALONG FOR THE RIDE, A LOW-LYING FOG, QUICK & DIRTY (A SUBWAY FANTASY),* and *THE FERRY* must give credit to the Author of the Play in all programs distributed in connection with performances of the Play, and in all instances in which the title of the Play appears for the purposes of advertising, publicizing or otherwise exploiting the Play and/or a production. The name of the Author *must* appear on a separate line on which no other name appears, immediately following the title and *must* appear in size of type not less than fifty percent of the size of the title type.

TABLE OF CONTENTS

LEAVING TANGIER

by

David Johnston

LEAVING TANGIER was originally produced by Blue Coyote Theater Group—Kyle Ancowitz, Robert Buckwalter, Gary Shrader, and Stephen Speights—at the Abingdon Theater in New York City, with the following cast:

COOPER	Bruce Barton
ROSEMUND SNODDY	Jonna McElrath
REVEREND BESTERMAN	Gary Shrader
TAP	Carter Jackson

The production was directed by Gary Shrader; Set and Lighting Design by Chris Jones; Costumes by Carrie Worthley; Sound Design by Connor McGibboney. The first performance was on May 22, 2003.

CHARACTERS

COOPER: Early forties. Male. Poet, teacher and translator who left America twenty years ago and now resides in Tangier. Devoted to the memory of his friend, the writer Oswin Everett Pickett.

ROSEMUND SNODDY *(pronounced with hard "o")*: Early thirties, female. Very Southern. A fierce defender of her family and their good name.

REVEREND DON BESTERMAN: Male. Any age. Genial and unassuming. A born peacemaker.

TAP SNODDY: Late teens – early twenties, male. Rosemund's brother. Eager, excitable and conflicted.

(A graveyard. Summer. COOPER, a man in his early forties, is seated on a stone bench. He wears a light summer suit and a hat, as if dressed for the tropics. There is an elegant walking stick on the ground by his side. He is engrossed in a book. A woman in her thirties enters. She wears a flowered dress, white gloves and a summer hat, suitable for church. Her manner is wrathful and her Southern drawl is unapologetic. This is ROSEMUND SNODDY. She removes her gloves when she starts to speak and places them in her purse. She is accompanied by a smiling, benign presence, the REVEREND DON BESTERMAN. BESTERMAN carries a Bible.)

ROSEMUND. *(Removing her gloves.)* Are you him?
COOPER. *(Startled.)* Oh, God.
ROSEMUND. Are you him?
COOPER. You scared me. I didn't think there was anyone else out here.
ROSEMUND. Are you him?
COOPER. Him who?
ROSEMUND. Him. The friend. Uncle Oswin's friend. From Algeria.
COOPER. Tangier. I'm from Tangier. Algeria's a different place.
ROSEMUND. Are you him?
COOPER. Yes.

(COOPER slowly gets to his feet, reaching for his cane.)

ROSEMUND. What's wrong with your leg?
COOPER. What do you mean?
ROSEMUND. You walk with a stick. Are you crippled?
COOPER. No.
ROSEMUND. Do you have polio? You shouldn't be ashamed if you have polio.

COOPER. Polio?

ROSEMUND. My Uncle Frank had polio. One leg's an inch shorter than the other. It's not noticeable, he just has to buy special shoes.

BESTERMAN. He's much too young to have had polio.

ROSEMUND. I guess you're right.

COOPER. I don't have polio.

ROSEMUND. Why do you walk with a stick then?

COOPER. They wouldn't let me bring a gun into the airport. Who are you?

ROSEMUND. I'm Rosemund Snoddy. This is Reverend Besterman. He's the preacher here at Muddy Brook United Methodist.

BESTERMAN. God bless you, sir.

COOPER. Hi.

ROSEMUND. I'm Orrie Mae's granddaughter. She was Orrie Mae Pickett. Uncle Oswin's sister.

COOPER. How did you know...?

ROSEMUND. She couldn't come today. She's in the home. Not with the program, as they say. And Momma—my momma, Miz Bernice Snoddy—she died of cancer five years ago. Grandma Orrie Mae and Uncle Oswin hadn't spoken in forty years. The last time she saw him was their daddy's funeral. Uncle Oswin called her a harpy. He said a-very-bad-word you, you harpy. That's what she told me. I had to look up harpy, I didn't know what a harpy was. I found a picture of a big ugly woman with sagging boobs and wings like a bat. That's the last time they spoke.

COOPER. I see.

ROSEMUND. He was a very wicked man, my Uncle Oswin. Nasty. *(She points to the carry-on bag.)* Is that him?

COOPER. *(Glancing at the bag.)* Oh, yes.

ROSEMUND. Is that all of him?

COOPER. Unless he's spilled during the flight.

BESTERMAN. Orrie Mae. Rosemund's grandmother. She's a fine woman. Made me feel very welcome when I came here to Muddy Brook five years ago. Fine woman. Everybody calls her Miss Orrie.

ROSEMUND. You haven't told us your name.

COOPER. Cooper. My name is Cooper.

ROSEMUND. Are you a writer as well, Mr. Cooper?

COOPER. Yes. Not in the same league with Oswin, though.

ROSEMUND. Yes. Well. Some people seem to like his books.

COOPER. Do you like them?

ROSEMUND. You couldn't pay me to read that filth, Mr. Cooper. We appreciate your bringing Uncle Oswin all this way. It was very gracious of you. You must be eager to return to Tangier.

COOPER. You have no idea.

ROSEMUND. When are you returning?

COOPER. I have a room in Charlottesville tonight, tomorrow I fly back to Kennedy in New York, and from there to Tangier.

ROSEMUND. I'm sorry you won't be able to see more of Junction Bluffs.

BESTERMAN. We're not far from some wonderful Civil War battlefields. Very interesting. Historically.

COOPER. Maybe next time.

BESTERMAN. Yes.

ROSEMUND. Well, thank you for all your help, Mr. Cooper. We're very grateful to you. We'll take it from here.

COOPER. You'll—?

ROSEMUND. You're welcome to stay for the service if you like.

COOPER. What service?

ROSEMUND. The funeral.

BESTERMAN. The funeral.

ROSEMUND. The service. For Uncle Oswin.

BESTERMAN. For the deceased.

COOPER. And what will be happening at this funeral?

ROSEMUND. What will be happening? It's a funeral. The preacher will speak...

BESTERMAN. That's me.

ROSEMUND. A few prayers. Then we'll bury the uh ....

COOPER. The urn?

ROSEMUND. Yes. The urn. The ashes. Maybe a hymn.

COOPER. Hmm. No.

ROSEMUND. Well, I'm sorry you won't be able to stay, but perhaps it's appropriate for only blood relations to be ....

COOPER. No. Rosemund. I was not talking about my travel plans. I was saying, no, Rosemund, there will be no funeral service. Oswin Everett Pickett's will—of which I am the executor—is very explicit. No funeral. No religious observance. Just the urn and a few small items, in the family plot. He was a devout atheist and the will is very clear on that point.

ROSEMUND. I would like to see this will. As a blood relation, I believe I have that right.

COOPER. As a blood relation under Oswin Everett Pickett's will, you specifically have no rights. He was quite clear on that point too. I am the executor, the beneficiaries are—several young Arab men and a few universities. His personal papers have been deposited at the University of Texas, for scholarly research. A sum has been set aside for Muddy Brook Church for his interment and headstone—

BESTERMAN. We have a cemetery fund as well for upkeep and maintenance, you know, to keep the grass cut and looking nice—

COOPER. His copyrights are held in trust by his American publisher and they will be distributing any moneys to his—

ROSEMUND. This is just monstrous.

COOPER. To his beneficiaries. Beneficiaries. Not family. No service.

(Pause.)

BESTERMAN. Powerful hot today, Mr. Cooper. Must've brought this heat with you from Africa. Well, Rosemund, perhaps we should ....

ROSEMUND. And just what was your relationship with Uncle Oswin?

COOPER. I was his friend for the last twenty-two years.

ROSEMUND. Were you one of his boys?

COOPER. I was twenty-two years ago. Then I graduated to friend.

BESTERMAN. I should get inside. There's a Methodist Ladies Auxiliary meeting at—

ROSEMUND. Don, don't you move. And where are you from, sir?

COOPER. I'm from Tangier.

ROSEMUND. You don't look African. Where are your people from?

COOPER. Memphis.

ROSEMUND. Memphis?

COOPER. Yes.

ROSEMUND. That's where you grew up?

COOPER. Yes.

ROSEMUND. You don't sound like it.

COOPER. Thank you.

ROSEMUND. What compelled you to leave Memphis and go to Tangier, Mr. Cooper?

COOPER. Narcotics and sex with boys.

ROSEMUND. Having been to Memphis, I find it hard to believe you had to travel that far. So, Mr. Cooper. No money for the family. No funeral service. No nothing.

COOPER. That's correct.

ROSEMUND. Hardly seems fair, don't you think?

COOPER. It's not my decision. Those were Oswin's wishes. You still haven't told me how you knew I would be here.

ROSEMUND. My brother Tap, he's big into that internet. He found out Uncle Oswin died a few weeks ago. Did a little research, called the big New York publishing house, checked on a few international flights—there're not that many that connect to Charlottesville.

COOPER. That's an awful lot of checking to do to find out about someone you hated.

ROSEMUND. I don't hate, Mr. Cooper. Uncle Oswin is family. And I had a promise to keep.

COOPER. A promise? To whom? Oswin? You never met him.

ROSEMUND. No, I am not speaking about that evil old man. I'm talking about my grandmother.

BESTERMAN. Miss Orrie. Everyone calls her Miss Orrie.

ROSEMUND. You have no idea what it was like staying in this county and being a blood relation of the great Oswin Everett Pickett. Grandma Orrie practically married the first man who asked so she wouldn't be a Pickett anymore. She became a Snoddy. Forty years of grubby little graduate students with tape recorders, trying to find some great insight into that bastard's dope-addled mind by pestering my grandmother.

BESTERMAN. Rosemund, perhaps we'd better ....

ROSEMUND. Here she is, a good Methodist, a schoolteacher from one of the oldest families in the county, and Uncle Oswin is being denounced in the Senate as a Communist and a pederast and a dope fiend. Editorials in the paper in Richmond and Charlottesville, some of 'em in the Washington papers. Let me tell you, Mr. Cooper, it was only because of some very high connections that Grandma Orrie was not dismissed from the Daughters of the Confederacy.

COOPER. Lady, I don't care about any of this.

ROSEMUND. No, of course you don't. Nothing I'm talking about has ever been important to you. That man destroyed his family.

COOPER. Because he moved away and wrote some books?

ROSEMUND. Before Uncle Oswin, we had standing in this

community. We didn't have money, but we had position and respect. Then he put his perversions on display and held us up as a laughingstock. Everything the man touched smelled like a billy goat.

BESTERMAN. Rosemund, everyone thinks very highly of you and Tap and Miss Orrie. Nobody blames you for your uncle. This woman, Mr. Cooper, her father passed away years ago and she raised her little brother, nursed her mother up to her passing away, now she looks after her grandmother ....

ROSEMUND. Please, Don. My grandmother—a saint, Mr. Cooper, a saint—she told me many a time, many many a time— Rosemund, you've got to pray for your Uncle Oswin. We can't give up on him. He's family. No matter what happened to her, no matter what indignities she had heaped up on her because she was the sister of this wicked, wicked man—she always said, don't forget to pray for your Uncle Oswin.

BESTERMAN. A wonderful woman, Miss Orrie Mae. A pillar of faith in this community.

ROSEMUND. And do you know what else, Mr. Cooper?

BESTERMAN. A rock.

ROSEMUND. Yes, she is. And her whole life, she told me— Oswin will be back. He'll come back here to Junction Bluffs. He won't be buried someplace else. I know it. And if I'm not there, you've got to make sure he's buried proper, Rosemund.

COOPER. Oswin's will says no religious service. That was his wish. Not your grandmother's.

ROSEMUND. Oh, I didn't believe her. I told Grandmom she was crazy. I said, Uncle Oswin's never coming back, they're just gonna throw him out the back window of his big house in Africa and let the dogs go at him, like Jezebel in the Bible. But she said, no. He'll be back. And she was right. Here he is. Guess she knew him better than you did, Mr. Cooper. I'll tell you another thing. It makes no difference to me if the funeral's today or tomorrow or next week. I'm not taking orders from you or a can of dirt. This is what Grandmom wanted and I don't care if the old monster suffers the tortures of the damned, he's getting a good Methodist funeral.

BESTERMAN. Black gum against thunder. That's Rosemund.

(Pause.)

COOPER. What?

BESTERMAN. Black gum against thunder. It's an expression

Miss Orrie used to use, talking 'bout Rosemund here. Her granddaughter.

COOPER. What does it mean?

BESTERMAN. Black gum's a tree, Mr. Cooper. It resists lightning. Lightning'll take down any other tree. Elm. Oak. Pine. Not a black gum. Black gum'll take it. That's what Miss Orrie used to always say 'bout Rosemund here. Black gum against thunder. *(Pause.)* Meaning she knows her own mind. *(Pause.)* Mighty fine woman. Miss Orrie. *(Pause.)* Well, Rosemund, perhaps we'd better leave and let Mr. Cooper—

ROSEMUND. Yes, I believe I've said all I need to—

COOPER. Do you have any respect for the dead, Rosemund?

ROSEMUND. What a vulgar question.

COOPER. I don't know why he wanted to come back here.

ROSEMUND. Your manners. You've spent too long in the Dark Continent, Mr. Cooper.

COOPER . I don't know why he wanted me to bring him. Maybe he thought it would be fun for me to meet his family. Those are his wishes. He's your uncle. Will you abide by them?

(TAP bursts into the graveyard. He is in his early twenties and dressed in a white shirt and khaki pants.)

TAP. Is that him?

ROSEMUND. Tap, what the hell are you doing here?

TAP. That's him, isn't it? Are you Uncle Oswin's friend? Is that Uncle Oswin in the bag? Can I see him? You tried to do this without me, Rosemund! I told you I wanted to come!

BESTERMAN. Hello, Tap, how are you today?

ROSEMUND. Tap, you get back to the house right now! Aren't you supposed to be at work? You gonna be late for work!

TAP. Rosemund, I called at the Wal-Mart and I said I'd be in at five! I told 'em there was a family funeral. Is that Uncle Oswin in the bag?

COOPER. Yes.

TAP. Whoa. Can I see him?

ROSEMUND. Mr. Cooper doesn't have time for your foolishness, Tap.

COOPER. Sure. You can see him.

(COOPER gently takes the urn from the bag. He hands it to TAP.)

TAP. Whoa. This is him, isn't it?

COOPER. That's him.

TAP. He wrote *Lunch with Cannibals* and *Junkie Express* and *Peyote Nights* and *The Last Words of Mad Dog Coll*....

COOPER. You know his writing?

TAP. I've read every word, Mister.

ROSEMUND. He didn't get that filth from me.

TAP. Shit, Rosemund, they're just books.

ROSEMUND. Please don't swear in front of the preacher, Tap.

TAP. All I'm saying is ....

BESTERMAN. It's quite all right.

ROSEMUND. I don't approve of a lot of the things Tap reads. But he's not gonna listen to me. I'm just his sister.

TAP. Rosemund gets her panties in a bunch 'cause I read Uncle Oswin's books.

ROSEMUND. I loathe that expression.

BESTERMAN. I think it's great for young people to read. That's wonderful.

(ROSEMUND glares at BESTERMAN.)

ROSEMUND. Tap, this is Mr. Cooper. He's brought Uncle Oswin all the way from Tangier and now he's going back.

TAP. You're taking the ashes back to Tangier?

COOPER. No, I'm going back to Tangier. Oswin stays here.

TAP. Were you a friend?

COOPER. For twenty-two years.

TAP. What was he like? What's Tangier like? Was he mad when Gore Vidal sued him? Was he taking amphetamines the whole time he was writing *Palaces of Red Dust*?

COOPER. Every minute.

ROSEMUND. Yes, well, you see where all that drug taking got him, Tap. He's dead.

TAP. Shit, Rosemund, the man was eighty-seven.

ROSEMUND. Swearing in front of the preacher.

TAP. I'm just saying he was eighty-seven, it's not like he was ....

ROSEMUND. There is no need for you to pester Mr. Cooper. He's got things to do and then he's leaving. Unfortunately, Mr. Cooper will not be able to stay for the funeral. The service will be ... let's say tomorrow. Right, Reverend?

BESTERMAN. Of course.

ROSEMUND. Ten o'clock? I have some errands to run.

BESTERMAN. I wanted to get some fishing in. Me and Nash Pulliam. Could we do it at ....

ROSEMUND. Ten o'clock.

BESTERMAN. That'll be fine.

ROSEMUND. And Mr. Cooper will be returning to Tangier.

TAP. You're not staying for the funeral?

COOPER. No.

TAP. You came all this way and you're not staying for the funeral?

COOPER. Oswin didn't want a funeral service. He was not a religious man. Your sister has decided to go ahead and have one despite his wishes.

ROSEMUND. Tap, you need to get to work.

TAP. Uncle Oswin didn't want a service?

ROSEMUND. I said, you are gonna be late to work and we need that money and I will not have you losing that job to lollygag around the graveyard asking a lot of pointless questions. Go to work, Tap.

TAP. Why you gonna have preaching if the man said he didn't want it?

ROSEMUND. Are you gonna go to work?

TAP. I'll go when I'm ready. I wanna talk to Mr. Cooper.

ROSEMUND. Well, it is not my fault when the bills come due at the end of the month and there's no money to pay them because you lost your job.

TAP. *(Explodes at ROSEMUND.)* Rosemund, stop speaking to me like I'm a little kid. I said I want to talk to Mr. Cooper and I'll go to work when I'm good and goddamn ready.

(Pause.)

ROSEMUND. Well. I suppose there's nothing more I need to say. And I certainly don't want to stay here and be spoken to like this.

TAP. Go then.

ROSEMUND. Mr. Cooper. Thank you for all you have done for my family. I hope someday we can repay the favor. Let's go, Don.

(ROSEMUND turns to leave. BESTERMAN walks over to COOPER and shakes his hand.)

BESTERMAN. A pleasure to meet you, Mr. Cooper. Have a safe

flight back to Tangier.

COOPER. Thank you.

ROSEMUND. Come on, Don.

BESTERMAN. It's wonderful everyone wants to keep their promises.

ROSEMUND. Let's go, Don.

BESTERMAN. It's unfortunate when they don't line up.

ROSEMUND. *Don!*

(ROSEMUND stalks away and BESTERMAN follows.)

COOPER. She's your sister?

TAP. Yeah.

COOPER. She's a hag.

TAP. Rosemund's not bad. She's not. Although she gets me so mad sometimes I'd just as soon shoot her as look at her. But she's had it rough. She's had to take care of everyone. Her life's been real hard.

COOPER. Good.

TAP. She just gets crazy when it comes to Uncle Oswin. I swear, she blames him for the fact that she ain't married. But Rosemund and me … I mean, it's just the two of us since Momma died. We're all we've got.

COOPER. Sorry. She is your sister. I think this heat's getting to me. I'm used to dry heat.

(COOPER goes to the carry-on and brings out a small box.)

TAP. Uncle Oswin really didn't want a funeral?

COOPER. No. He wanted to be cremated; he wanted me to bring the ashes here to the family plot—all the way across the damn world. And no religion. Oswin had a thing about organized religion. It's all in the will.

TAP. Did you tell Rosemund that?

COOPER. Of course.

TAP. So why is she gonna have one?

COOPER. She said she promised your grandmother.

TAP. Oh.

COOPER. I think it's spite.

TAP. What are you doing with those things?

COOPER. Just a few items I wanted to leave.

TAP. What?

COOPER. A few personal things.

TAP. Do you want me to go? Do you want to be alone? Hey, what have you got there?

(COOPER pulls a book out of the box.)

COOPER. Know what this is?

(TAP takes the book.)

TAP. Holy shit. This is a first edition of *Lunch with Cannibals*.
COOPER. Look inside.

(TAP reads.)

TAP. Wow. He wrote that to you?
COOPER. Yes.
TAP. You're just gonna leave this on the grave?
COOPER. I don't need it anymore.
TAP. You could get five hundred bucks for this on ebay.
COOPER. I have no idea what an ebay is, so I'll just leave the book here.
TAP. Are you a writer, Mr. Cooper?
COOPER. Poetry. I teach at an American school in Tangier. I've translated several Arab poets.
TAP. Have I heard of you?
COOPER. No.
TAP. How come?
COOPER. I'm not very good. Nothing to compare with Oswin. Oswin—he was completely mad. I've known great talents before, but they usually make you feel small. Not your uncle. Just by knowing him, you felt gifted. Larger. Now he's gone and I see ... I'm a mediocre poet.
TAP. Oh, no, I bet you're ....
COOPER. I don't mind. Some are geniuses. Some bring the ashes in the carry-on bag. It's my privilege.
TAP. What do you do in Tangier?
COOPER. Read, write a bit, teach, translate, tea at Oswin's most afternoons. I don't know what I'll do with my afternoons now. Lots of hashish. I've accomplished ... very little in the last twenty-two years. *(COOPER sighs, reflects.)* It's been ... heaven.

TAP. Really?

COOPER. You have no idea how stressful it is to leave Tangier. I haven't left in twenty-two years. I left Memphis at nineteen for the summer. Decided to tour Europe. Took a detour into North Africa. I was set to return to Rhodes College and business school. I met Oswin, who was my idol. He invited me to his place for drinks. He insisted I try some of this great hash. I did. I took a nap. I woke up with him. I never left. It's been absolute, fucking heaven. So much fun you can't imagine.

(COOPER takes more objects from the bag.)

TAP. Did Uncle Oswin tell you what he wanted to be buried with?

COOPER. Some he requested. Some I added. Gitanes, his favorite cigarettes— *(COOPER tosses a pack of cigarettes on the ground.)* A handful of earth from Tangier. *(He places a vial of earth on the grave.)* Shell casings from his thirty ought six.

(COOPER drops a can of shell casings.)

TAP. He liked guns a lot, didn't he?

COOPER. Did he ever. He and William Burroughs loved to vanish into the desert for days to eat mushrooms and shoot lizards. And this— *(He holds up a photo.)* This is Ahmed.

(COOPER looks at TAP, hands him the photo.)

TAP. *(Staring at the picture.)* Whoa. *(Pause.)* Was Ahmed a friend?

COOPER. A very, very good friend.

TAP. *(Still staring at the picture.)* Did you know Ahmed?

COOPER. Everybody knew Ahmed.

(COOPER gently takes the picture from TAP and places it on the grave.)

TAP. Tell me everything about him. I want to know everything.

COOPER. Why are you interested?

TAP. Well, his books are amazing. There's that description of the desert and the Bedouins in *Lunch with Cannibals* and then it turns into this whole Arab warrior thing in the seventh century during the

Crusades. All that stuff linking cannibalism and communion and um um ....

COOPER. Sex?

TAP. Yeah. Those warriors and sex. I mean, that's intense stuff. I never got stuff like that in high school. They wanted us to read freaking Silas Marner. Freaking Song of Hiawatha bullshit. Oswin was cool. You know what I loved about him, Mr. Cooper?

COOPER. It's just Cooper.

TAP. It's not your last name?

COOPER. It's my first.

TAP. What I loved about him. Why I wish I'd met him. Was when he tore up the maps.

COOPER. What do you mean?

TAP. When he tore up the maps. That part in *Peyote Nights* when they're in the jungle and they tear up their maps 'cause they've decided they're going to find their own way out and they know they might die but they do it anyway. That was him. That's what he did. With his own life. I mean, everything is mapped out here. Your whole life. Know what I mean?

COOPER. Explain it to me.

TAP. Me and Rosemund, we live in Grandmom's house—where Uncle Oswin lived when he was a kid. Daddy died when we were kids and Momma died of breast cancer five years ago and we check in on Grandmom at the home. And I finished high school and Rosemund says, OK, Tap, it's the Army or a job, there's no money for college. So I went to work for the Wal-Mart and I became assistant manager of the hardware department and now I'm up for assistant store manager and that training takes eleven weeks and everyone is happy 'cause I'm advancing in the organization and everyone at work is nice all the time, 'cause—you know—it's Wal-Mart. And I'll get married in a coupla years, 'cause—you know—you get married. And I'll have kids and buy a little house in Powhatan and get fat and work at Wal-Mart and the car'll break down all the time and Rosemund'll hate my wife no matter who she is, she's just gonna hate her and my kids won't talk to me and I'll look at the TV and maybe my wife'll leave me and I'll start drinking late at night by myself in the garage, drinking bourbon out of little Styrofoam cups late at night in the garage and then I'll fall down and need a new hip or get senile and go into the home or just die. *(Pause.)* I'm sorry, Mr. Cooper, what was your question?

COOPER. That's all right.

TAP. I lost my train of thought.

COOPER. You answered the question, don't worry.

TAP. But Uncle Oswin wasn't having any of that. He ran away and wrote these amazing books and experimented with drugs and knew everyone and had all these lovers.

(TAP has been looking at the objects on the grave. He picks up the photo and stares at it.)

COOPER. It was all a huge joke to Oswin. Everything. Which is also probably why he sent me across the planet to dump him. Son of a bitch. Probably thought it would be funny. No other reason why I should be here. *(Pause.)* Come with me.

TAP. What?

COOPER. Come with me. To Tangier.

TAP. Oh.

COOPER. Go home. Pack what you like. Meet me at the airport tomorrow. Come with me.

TAP. I can't go, Mr. Cooper.

COOPER. Just Cooper. Why not?

TAP. I'm not like my uncle. I can't run away and be interesting.

COOPER. Come with me.

TAP. I can't. I'm starting training for assistant store manager and that takes eleven weeks.

COOPER. Come with me, Tap.

TAP. There's a leak in the basement by the ping-pong table and Nash Pulliam says it might be cracks in the foundation so I have to get that fixed.

COOPER. Screw the ping-pong table.

TAP. It's the floor.

COOPER. Screw that too. Come with me.

TAP. I have to get the leaves off the roof or the gutters fill up and collapse.

COOPER. Let 'em fall. Come with me.

TAP. There's Sonny Boy.

COOPER. Who's Sonny Boy?

TAP. He's Grandmom's dog, he's a bluetick hound and he's fourteen and he doesn't see very good and he has arthritis in his hips and if I don't put the food in his bowl, he won't eat 'cause he don't like Rosemund. He sleeps in the yard all day, but he wakes up when he hears my car. I can't go.

(Pause.)

COOPER. I'm all finished here. I should be off to the hotel.
TAP. It was nice meeting you.
COOPER. Likewise. Here.

(COOPER picks up the signed book and hands it to TAP.)

TAP. Are you sure?
COOPER. It's mine. I'll do with it what I like.
TAP. Wow. It's just … thanks.
COOPER. You're welcome. Don't sell it to an ebay.
TAP. I won't.
COOPER. Oh. Wait.

(COOPER takes the book back from TAP, picks up the photo of Ahmed from the grave, tucks it into the book and gives it back to TAP.)

TAP. Whydja gimme that?
COOPER. Thought you might like it. To remember your uncle.

(Pause.)

TAP. Thanks. *(TAP chuckles.)* Rosemund would have a stroke if she saw this.
COOPER. Then tape it to the bathroom mirror.
TAP. I should go. I'm gonna be late for work.
COOPER. Don't want that.
TAP. Thanks. For everything. I'll talk to Rosemund about the funeral service.
COOPER. That's nice of you.
TAP. I mean, he's our uncle and that's what he wanted, right?
COOPER. Right.
TAP. So I'll tell her no. *(Here his thought breaks off.)* Bye.

(TAP runs off. COOPER watches him go. Silence. He kneels by the grave, arranges his few items. He is still. He lowers his head silently, almost as if praying.)

THE END

PROPS

COOPER
Travel bag containing:
    Book (first edition of *Lunch with Cannibals* by Oswin Everett
      Pickett)
    Jar of earth
    Pack of *Gitanes* cigarettes
    Metal canister of shell casings
    Photograph of Ahmed

REVEREND BESTERMAN
Bible

COSTUMES

COOPER
Beige linen suit with dark green short sleeve shirt
Beige and brown two-toned shoes with silk socks
Brown belt
Straw hat
Walking cane
Sunglasses

ROSEMUND
Navy floral print dress (dated)
Navy low heel shoes and light-colored stockings
Navy sunhat
Navy clutch purse
White gloves

REVEREND BESTERMAN
Dark brown slacks and light blue short-sleeved cotton shirt
White t-shirt
Suspenders
Brown fedora-style hat
Brown shoes and dark socks

TAP
Khaki pants and white button-down, long sleeved cotton shirt
Brown belt
Brown shoes and dark socks

BLUEBERRY WALTZ

by

Liz Amberly

With thanks to Scott Sickles
With love to Greg

BLUEBERRY WALTZ was first produced by The WorkShop Theater Company in New York for the Short Play Festival on July 26, 2003. It was directed by Doug Moser. The cast was as follows:

DEB   Danielle Di Vecchio
KEITH   Jeff Watkins

ABOUT THE AUTHOR

Liz Amberly's plays have been performed and developed at The Pulse Theatre, The Workshop Theater, Epiphany Theater, Word of Mouth and American Theater for Actors. She is a member of the Dramatists Guild and has a Post-Graduate Certificate from the London Academy of Music and Dramatic Art and a B.F.A in Music/Theater from Syracuse University. Her other one-acts include *Asking Price, Dream Vacation, The Dedication* and *Double Whammy*. She has several full-length plays, including the drama *Whisper Down the Lane*. She was commissioned by the Harriet Beecher Stowe Center to co-write a multi-media play for school tours. She also co-created *Time Zone*, an original TV series for 'tweens.

CHARACTERS

DEB: 30-40, a homemaker
KEITH: 30-40, a coal miner

SETTING

Rural Pennsylvania. The present.

All of the action takes place in Keith and Deb's kitchen. There is a well-worn sturdy kitchen table center, and there are some chairs and a side table nearby.

(Lights rise on a simple rural kitchen filled with handmade decorations.

DEB, wearing pajamas, is standing over the kitchen table, breaking eggs and stirring batter in a mixing bowl with a wooden spoon. There are measuring cups, flour and a coffee pot on a side table. KEITH enters.)

KEITH. You don't have to—

DEB. I already started.

KEITH. Toast is fine, honey. Really. I said that.

DEB. You love waffles.

KEITH. But you don't have to make them every day.

DEB. I want to make them every—

KEITH. Just sometimes. Whenever you feel up to it. Now and then would be fine.

DEB. No, I was just too lazy to make them. That's what you said.

KEITH. I didn't mean—

DEB. A good breakfast. I'm just doing that.

KEITH. I like cereal.

DEB. Not as much as waffles. *(DEB continues to prepare the batter. KEITH finds a shoe under the table and another one across the floor. He sits in a chair to put them on. DEB gets out a basket of blueberries.)* You want blueberry today or just plain?

KEITH. You made blueberry yesterday.

DEB. 'Cause they're your favorite.

KEITH. But I thought you used 'em up.

DEB. Bought more.

KEITH. Bought more blueberries? When?

DEB. Yesterday.

KEITH. You can't keep making blueberry waffles everyday.

DEB. Yes I—

KEITH. Not every day!!!

DEB. *(A pause, then—)* So plain then. I won't put in any blueberries. I just thought you liked blueberries, but I won't put any in.

KEITH. Honey, it's great that you're feeling industrious, but you've already got your hands full. Don't you have to get the kids ready?

DEB. They like waffles, too.

KEITH. They'd like bubble gum for breakfast if you let them have it. They don't care what you make, so don't spend the time. You have their lunches to get ready and their backpacks and their notes for school ....

DEB. They can't learn on an empty stomach.

KEITH. Their stomachs aren't empty from eating cereal. And it's fortified, right? I think it's healthier than waffles, and you're always worried about everybody's health. Even the Surgeon General says people should eat more cereal everyday. Natural grains or something. You were doing a good thing for the kids. Giving them cereal.

DEB. Just keep everybody fed, I figured. But I never made waffles, 'cause it was just too much of a pain in the neck to get out the waffle iron, and keep it clean, and store the cord, and make the batter. And here you were heading down to the mines everyday, risking your life, and I had to say "make yourself some cereal" like I couldn't even pour the milk.

KEITH. But you made the toast—

DEB. —You don't like toast.

KEITH. But it's okay with jam. And you always got me strawberry.

DEB. Store-bought. Like if I go to the store and buy you a jar, you should be happy.

KEITH. I was happy.

DEB. You were never happy.

KEITH. I should have been ecstatic. Hey, just look at me sitting here. I thank God for letting me sit at this table and eat anything in the world. Anything.

(A beat.)

DEB. Do you know what I thought?

KEITH. When?

DEB. Do you know what I thought, when I stood there with the other wives, and the kids ... watching the police ....

KEITH. Don't keep thinking about the terrible part. It's over now.

DEB. But what do you think I thought?

KEITH. I know. You thought I was gone.

DEB. No.

KEITH. Good. 'Cause I wasn't.

DEB. And then they got the telephone down that pipe, and at least we find out that you guys are okay down there ....

KEITH. ...See ....

DEB. ... Well, so far, at that point. But then Joe says on the phone to the police that you guys had been writing letters to your loved ones. That in case you didn't make it, you wanted us to know what you were thinking in those last moments.

KEITH. Made good sense rather than just sit there.

DEB. But do you know what I thought?

KEITH. That I could still die, even after you heard my voice on the phone?

DEB. No. I thought that if you died, I didn't want to read your letter.

KEITH. Didn't want to?

DEB. If anything happened, I never ever would read it.

KEITH. You wouldn't read my letter?

DEB. I thought about what you might write. And all I could think—of all the things there are to think in the whole wide world at that moment—all I could think is that maybe all you could think to write was "See ... guess you should've made me more waffles."

KEITH. What?...

DEB. ... And I swore to myself that if you ever made it out. If you were alive and okay, I would make you waffles every day of your life. I promised myself, and I made a pact with God.

KEITH. How could you possibly think ....

DEB. ... Because sometimes you realize that you were never really listening. In all that time you had, that you never heard a single word. That if somebody asks for waffles, it might just be that they like them and why isn't that okay? To give somebody something that they like that would only take five minutes out of your day. It should have been the first thing that happened every morning when you woke up, a breakfast of hot waffles, but it never happened that way. 'Cause somehow I thought it was too much trouble.

KEITH. I read to you the letter that I began ...

DEB. ... I know ....

KEITH. ... because you deserved to know what you meant to me, whether I made it out or not.

DEB. But when I read that letter, and the words that you picked were so beautiful ...

KEITH. ... probably spelled stuff wrong ....

DEB. ... I tried to figure out what did I do to deserve that letter, and I couldn't think of a single thing. What did I do?... Didn't even try. Didn't bother to pay attention. You worked so hard, and all those mornings. All those nights and days. I never made any effort to give you a single thing that you wanted in your life.

KEITH. You gave me everything that I wanted in my life.

DEB. And now I have you back again when it really might not have happened ...

KEITH. See it worked out okay.

DEB. ... and I can't have you ever think that I wouldn't take the time to make you waffles.

KEITH. Do you think that I want anything else than just being able to sit down to breakfast with you? Whatever it is. To hear our children getting ready for school. To know that their mother loves them. And me. And that we're all okay. That I could live like this every day, and never regret anything in my life.

DEB. The day you asked me to marry you, I thought I must be the luckiest person in the entire world. And last week, when you came out of that hole with barely more than a scratch, I couldn't believe that I could get so lucky twice. It just didn't seem fair, with so many unlucky people in the world, that I could get you twice.

KEITH. The man who complains about breakfast is your knight in shining armor?

DEB. Like a fairy tale.

KEITH. So maybe I should sweep you off your feet or something. Take you out. Go dancing one night.

DEB. Oh, please ... you hate dancing.

KEITH. Hey, I got used to toast and cereal. I could get used to just about anything. So, what do you say?

DEB. You're not even serious.

KEITH. I bet McGovern's still has your favorite table in that corner near the band.

DEB. We can't just show up there.

KEITH. Sure we can.

DEB. We've got the kids.

KEITH. My mom'll watch them.

DEB. I don't have anything to wear.

KEITH. *(Teasing her.)* So, now you're trying to wrangle a shopping trip out of me?

DEB. No, I just mean—

KEITH. — How about a new dress?

DEB. I'm not trying to—

KEITH. A dancing dress and some new shoes from Coopers or someplace. I think that would be the perfect beginning for a night on the town. And then we'll head to McGovern's. Have a drink. Pretend we're teenagers.

DEB. I'm not going to pretend that I'm a teenager.

KEITH. Okay. Twenties then. Hanging out with the gang. Trying to catch each other's attention on the center of the floor. I'll wear something decent. And I won't get tired of dancing, I swear. How about it?

DEB. You don't have to.

KEITH. I know I don't. But I've been practicing some moves, and I want to try them out. Here, you wanna see?

(He turns on the stereo and begins doing some silly dancing moves.)

DEB. You're crazy.

KEITH. You bet.

(He continues to dance, taking her hands to join him.)

DEB. The kids are almost up.

KEITH. So they'll see how ol' Mom and Dad can still boogie down. Some entertainment with their breakfast.

DEB. I can just see them roll their eyes.

KEITH. Just wait till Saturday. We'll let the whole town see us on our big night out. We'll take over the dance floor at McGovern's and let them all shake their heads in horror at the spectacle of it all.

(The dancing gets bigger, and she gets caught up in his silliness. Then—)

DEB. Honey, you should stop. *(He doesn't.)* No, stop, really. Keith. You're supposed to be taking it easy.

KEITH. This is easy.

DEB. You could hurt yourself.

KEITH. I feel fine.

DEB. What if you start wheezing again? You have to stop. This isn't funny! *(Turning off the music.)* You're not supposed to be jumping around until you see the doctor again.

KEITH. I don't care about the doctor.

DEB. You should!

KEITH. I just want to take my wife out on a date.

DEB. Oh, so you can push yourself before you're ready? Get hurt? Have more of those dizzy spells because of me? And then you'll wonder why I can't ever just let you lie on the couch and take a nap? Why I can't just be happy just to have you hang out with me at home? … How's your body supposed to recover when you're doing all this stuff for me? The whole reason they told you to skip work this week was cause your body needs to recover, and here you were fixing my cabinets and working on the sink, and now you think I'm going to let you take me dancing? I don't want to go dancing!

KEITH. You think I'm some invalid now? That I can't pick up a tool or go hear some music? You think I'm gonna tip-toe around for the rest of my life? Sit in a chair 'cause I had an accident one day? Maybe I want to go dancing. Maybe all your talk of that silly ballroom class has gotten me in the mood. Maybe I want to see what all the fuss is about.

DEB. I won't make a fuss anymore. I promise.

KEITH. And what are you still worried about anyway? I mean, look at this.… (Picking up the newspaper from the table.) What are you reading?

DEB. It's the newspaper.

KEITH. It's the obituaries. This is how you start the day now?

DEB. It's just that—

KEITH. It's over. I'm fine. Honey, I just want you to come dancing with me. And you know how my mom will spoil the kids; they'll love it. Besides, I'm ready for some exercise. If you keep making me eat blueberry waffles soaked in butter and syrup, I've got to work them off somehow. So what do you say? (She doesn't answer, but instead goes back to her batter, stirring earnestly.) Deb ….

DEB. I just want you to have what you want. For breakfast, or dinner, or whatever. I could make you something else if you're tired of waffles. Oatmeal or pancakes or something.

KEITH. How about toast and cereal tomorrow. I'm kinda starting to miss it.

DEB. … Okay.

KEITH. And honey, Saturday … I'm serious.… A shopping trip and a night out on the town. My chance to be seen with my beautiful wife, and your chance to be seen with a charming, healthy, lucky guy who even arranges babysitting. (DEB is intent on her batter, but he *comes and takes the bowl away.)* I'll take it easy. I'll drink lots of water and rest when I need to. Maybe I'll tip the guy in the band to play some extra slow dances. You can show me some steps you've been learning from your class, and I even promise not to step on your feet. How's that?... Hey, offers to go out with me don't come along everyday you know, so you better take it while you can. *(He turns on a slow song, an old favorite.)* What do you say?

(She nods her head, too moved to answer. They embrace, then he takes her into a close dancing stance and begins to dance her around the kitchen. Music swells in the background, and the lights fade to black.)

THE END

COSTUME PLOT

Deb is wearing pajamas and slippers
Keith has casual clothes and a pair of shoes

PROPERTY PLOT

Mixing bowl
Wooden spoon
Coffee pot
Coffee cups
Measuring cup
Flour
Eggs
Waffle iron
Blueberries
Newspaper

SET DRAWING

ALONG
FOR THE RIDE

by

Jay D. Hanagan

ALONG FOR THE RIDE was originally produced by the Gatesinger Co. Ltd. on August 2, 2002 at Gates Hall in Pultneyville, NY, and was directed by Jay D. Hanagan. The cast, in order of appearance, was as follows:

CABBIE	Mike Mulberry
KERRIE	Nicole Stiokas
KARL	Andrew Meyer
KERRIE2	Sara Blankenberg
KARL2	David Meyer

For the Samuel French Off-Off-Broadway Festival Plays, Twenty Eighth Series, the work was produced by Armory Square Playhouse of Syracuse, NY (David Feldman, Artistic Director). The Technical Director was Margaret E. Hall and the entire production was directed by Mark Hessler with the following cast:

CABBIE	Carl Schwaber
KERRIE	April Pressel
KARL	Michael Haddad
KERRIE2	Lea Contarino
KARL2	Michael Steven Costello

(Swings: Penny Frank, Jay D. Hanagan,
Brian Neuls, Catherine Zapanta)

CHARACTERS

KERRIE: A woman.
KARL: A man.
KERRIE2: A woman's subconscious.
KARL2: A man's subconscious.
CABBIE: A cab driver.

SCENE

The illusion of a taxi cab.

TIME

Present day. New York City

(SETTING: We have a bare stage except for some chairs. These will be our taxicab. The "back seat" will be elevated slightly to catch the character's action there. When KERRIE2 and KARL2 enter, THEY will be dressed just like their conscious counterparts.

AT RISE: The CABBIE is sitting in his cab. KERRIE and KARL enter running from opposite sides.)

KERRIE. *(Calling out.)* Hold that cab!

KARL. *(Calling out.)* Cab! Cabbie! *(They both reach the cab and the door handle at the same time, and they both like what they see.)* Share?

KERRIE. I'm going— *(Pointing.)* —that way.

KARL. I am too.

CABBIE. Ain't none of us goin' anywhere 'til one of ya get in the cab!

KARL. *(Getting in.)* Park & 57th.

KERRIE. *(Getting in.)* I'm going to Madison.

KARL. Hey, close enough then.

(KERRIE2 and KARL2 enter from the same side as and stand directly behind their conscious counterparts as the cab starts moving.)

KERRIE2. What am I gonna do at Madison & 57th? Is Buccellati's still there? I could maybe put a down payment on a silver spoon.

KARL2. Wow. She's really pretty.

KERRIE2. He's got a nice smile.

KARL. Hi. My name is Karl.

KARL2. Okay. Good opening. You can't go wrong using the basics.

KERRIE. Is that a Karl with a "C" or a "K"?

KERRIE2. That was brilliant!

KARL2. Okay, so she may not be the brightest crayon in the box.

KARL. It's Karl with a "K."

KERRIE. Oh.

KERRIE2. "Oh"? Is that the best you can come up with? Look at him. The man already thinks you're "special"!

KARL. Do *you* have a name?

KERRIE. What? Oh. Of course I do.

KARL2. We're making real headway here.

KARL. Is it a secret?

KERRIE. Is what a secret?

KERRIE2. No no no no *no!*

KERRIE. Oh my name. No. It's not a secret.

KARL2. Try one more time.

KARL. Then what is it?

KERRIE. What?

KARL2. *(Shouting.)*	KERRIE2. *(Shouting.)*
Your name!	Your name!

KERRIE. It's Kerrie! *(Quietly.)* With a "K."

KARL. *(Extends hand.)* So, hello Kerrie with a "K." Pleased to meet you.

KERRIE. *(Shaking hands.)* Pleased to meet you, Karl. With a "K."

KARL2. Oh great. My hand is sweating. Maybe she won't notice.

KERRIE2. My hand is ice cold.

KARL2. Her hand is nice and cool.

KERRIE2. His hand is ... he's sweating.

KARL2. I think she noticed.

KERRIE2. He's nervous.

KARL2. Don't let her know you're nervous.

KERRIE2. So this must mean he doesn't think I'm a total loser.

KERRIE. So Karl.

KARL. Yes Kerrie.

KERRIE. Do you work in the city, or do you live around here too?

KARL. Connecticut. I take the train in.

(KERRIE lets go of his hand.)

KERRIE2. He's married.

KARL2. Oh no! She thinks you're married! Say something!

KARL. My family is there. I grew up there.

KERRIE2. Worse. He lives with his mother.

KARL2. Good move Einstein. Now she probably thinks you live with your mother.

KARL. I, uh ... I live alone. *(Both laugh nervously.)* My mother, she uh, she passed away not too awful long ago, actually.

KERRIE. I'm sorry to hear that.

KERRIE2. Hurdle number one cleared.

KARL2. How could I just kill off Mother like that?

KARL. It was a blessing really. Father's doing well though.

KERRIE. Is he in Connecticut?

KARL. Connecticut is where he calls home. He's semi-retired, although he's on a business trip right now.

KARL2. He's got his secretary with him, so I guess we can call it a business trip.

KERRIE. Oh? Where's he at?

KARL. In the south—

KARL2. —of France.

KARL. He always comes home as quick as he can though.

KARL2. It's Mother's money, after all.

KARL. So, do you live all alone in the big bad city?

KERRIE. I'm on the island.

KERRIE2. Coney Island.

KARL2. Long Island. Good. Her family has money. That will make Mother happy.

KARL. Where on Long Island? We have friends there.

KERRIE2. Friends?! Change the subject! Change the subject!

KERRIE. So, what brings you into the city?

KARL2. Boredom.

KARL. Business. You?

KERRIE. Business.

KERRIE2. Shopping. But not on Fifth.

KARL. You have beautiful eyes.

KARL2. What are you doing!? I was just thinking that! You weren't supposed to say it!

KERRIE. *(Embarrassed.)* Thank you. So do you.

KERRIE2. You weren't supposed to say that!

KARL2. Should I tell her I wear contacts?

KERRIE. *(Trying to change the subject.)* What about the rest of your family?

KARL. They have nice eyes too.

KARL2. Weak! Dweeb! Lame alert! *(KERRIE laughs a little.)* She's laughing? Okay then, let's run with it.

KARL. The rest of my family? It's just me actually.

KARL2. Great. First you kill off Mother, now Brenda and Bill.

KERRIE2. Thanksgiving will be easy.

KARL2. Thanksgiving is going to be hell.

KERRIE. So, you're an only child then.

KARL. Just me and the folks.

KERRIE. The folks?

KARL. I mean, me and Pops.

KARL2. Sorry.

KARL. How about you?

KERRIE. I have five brothers and sisters.

KARL. Five!?

KERRIE. Mom and Dad were nothing if not prolific.

KERRIE2. What the hell does that mean?

KARL. That's great to have so many brothers and sisters. I think it's just great.

KERRIE. Do you really?

KARL. Sure. I wish I had some brothers and sisters.

KARL2. So does Brenda and Bill.

KERRIE. Coming from a large family has its good points.

KERRIE2. Like moving out.

KARL2. Okay. We've gone as far as we can go on this family thing. Let's move on.

KARL. I've always wished I had come from a larger family.

KARL2. This is moving on?

KARL. I love kids.

KERRIE. So do I.

KERRIE2. Yeah ... for *break*fast! What are you *saying*?! You're the oldest of six! You're sick of kids!

KARL2. Earth to Stephen Hawkings! Now that's she's expecting a large family, how do you tell her you're sterile?

KARL. *(Changes subject.)* So you're in for business?

KERRIE. Yes, that's right.

KARL. What business are you in?

KERRIE2. What did he say?

KERRIE. *(To KARL.)* What business am I in?

KERRIE2. Thank you.

KARL. *(Nods.)* Hmm-mm.

KERRIE. Uh, clothes.

KARL. Oh really? Are you a model?

KARL2. Oh that's good!

KERRIE2. I could probably find my way to pushing out a couple of kids for this guy on that one line alone.

KERRIE. *(Giggle.)* What? Me? A model? Nooo! Me? Oh you're ... nooo!

KARL. So what do you do with clothes, besides wear them?

KERRIE. I uh ... I uh ....

KERRIE2. Don't you dare say "sell"! And don't you dare say "Gap."

KERRIE. I'm a buyer.

KARL. For who?

KERRIE2. Uh-oh.

KERRIE. For who?

KARL. Who do you buy for?

KERRIE. I'm freelance.

KARL2. Which means she sells knock-offs from the back of her van.

KERRIE. With all the down-sizing, there's a lot of us freelancing now.

KARL2. Okay, that sounds reasonable.

KERRIE2. "Down-sizing." Yes! Thank God for "20-20"!

KARL. That's very interesting. So I suppose you do a lot of traveling.

KARL2. She's probably just another rich, spoiled world traveler.

KERRIE. Oh, you know, here and there.

KARL. France? Italy?

KERRIE2. Little Italy.

KERRIE. Let's just say I prefer to stay close to home.

KERRIE2. Oh really?

KARL2. Oh really?

KARL. Oh really?

KERRIE. Really. Although I think I might enjoy traveling abroad more if I had a suitable companion to do it with.

KERRIE2. Or anyone at all who would pay.

KERRIE. What business are you in town for, Karl?

KARL2. She had to ask.

KARL. What business you say?

KERRIE. Yes.

KARL2. Stall her while I think of something besides how much I like to walk by the window at Victoria's Secret.

KARL. I lied, I'm not in town for business.

KARL2. That's not what I meant!

KERRIE. You're not?

KARL2. Okay ... okay ... something's coming ... give me half a sec....

KARL. No, I'm not.

KERRIE. A man of mystery, huh?

KARL2. Okay, let's go with that.

KARL. I'm really not allowed to talk much about it.

KERRIE. I'm intrigued. Or are you just teasing me?

KERRIE2. Or is he out on parole? Listen Sweetheart, you buy into that and you are on your own.

KARL2. I don't know what to do.

KARL. Would I tease you?

KERRIE. *(Smiling.)* Yes.

KARL2. *(Tosses a coin, looks at the result.)* Hmm!

KARL. You're right. I'm teasing.

KERRIE2. Okay, so he *won't* tell you what he does. So that makes him what? A con man? A pervert?

KARL. My family has money.

KERRIE2. A keeper?

KARL. I'm independently wealthy. I don't do much of anything, I'm afraid.

KERRIE2. *(Pleased.)* Rich with a dead mother.

KARL. And I haven't been totally honest with you on other things.

KERRIE2. Uh-oh. Mother's back on life support.

KARL2. What are you doing?! Honesty doesn't work!

KARL. I have a brother and a sister who are two of my best friends. My mother's alive and doing very well and my father's in France with his secretary doing even better.

KERRIE. Oh.

KERRIE2. Uh-oh.

KARL. I don't know why I lied earlier.

KERRIE2. So do we tell him the truth now?

KARL. And you've been so sweet and open and honest.

KERRIE2. We do *not* tell him the truth now.

KARL. Actually, what I wanted to say was ... no ... never mind.

KERRIE2. What?

KERRIE. What?

KARL. What I was about to say will sound so phony that you would never believe it anyway.

KERRIE2. Try me.

KERRIE. Try me.

KARL2. You're still on your own. You never listen to me anyway.

KARL. Well, when I first held your hand, *(Holds her hand.)* and looked into your eyes, *(Looks into her eyes.)* I ... I ....

CABBIE. Here we are. That'll be four fifty. Which one is coughin' up the fare? The blue-eyed goddess or the momma's boy?

KERRIE2. We're here already? Do something!

KARL2. Think you idiot think! Oh wait. That's my job!

KERRIE. *(Blurts out.)* I don't buy clothes, I sell them. At the Gap. *(Grabs KARL's hand and turns his head back towards her.)* You were about to say something.

CABBIE. He can tell you how much he lo-oves you after someone gives me four fifty plus a generous tip for the insulin I'm gonna have to get 'cause I'm getting a sugar overload here!

KARL. *(To CABBIE.)* Why don't you just mind your own beeswax!

KERRIE2. Beeswax?

KARL2. Beeswax?

KARL. *(To KERRIE.)* I suppose this is where we split up.

KERRIE2. Oh no!

KARL2. My one big chance and I blew it!

KERRIE. *(Letting go of his hand.)* I ... I suppose it is.

KARL. *(Gets an idea!; pulls out a money clip.)* All I have is a one and a one hundred.

KERRIE2. Ka-ching!

KARL2. No. Look in your wallet, there's—

CABBIE. —I can't break no Franklin!

KARL2. Oh, I get it. You're good!

KERRIE. *(Follows idea; looking in her purse.)* All I have is a dollar ... thirty-three cents in change ... and an old subway token. And Tic-tacs.

KERRIE2. You are so good!

CABBIE. Hey! What're the two of ya pullin' here?

KARL. I guess there's only one thing we can do.

KERRIE. What's that?

KARL. *(Tosses the hundred up to the CABBIE.)* Here. Let me know when we've used that up ... plus a generous tip.

CABBIE. Some days life is good.

KERRIE. So, where were we?

KARL.	KARL2
I'm sterile.	I'm sterile.
KERRIE.	KERRIE2
Oh thank God!	Oh thank God!

KARL. So, where were we?
KERRIE2. Take his hand.

(KERRIE takes KARL's hand as KERRIE2 takes KARL2's hand.)

KARL2. *(As he looks into KERRIE2's eyes.)* Look into her eyes.

(KARL looks into KERRIE's eyes.)

KERRIE. I think we were right here.
KERRIE2. Why aren't you kissing him?
KARL2. I hate to tell you this, Karl, but you're on your own.

(KARL2 and KERRIE2 start to kiss.)

KARL. Do you know what I have an overwhelming urge to do right now?
KERRIE. No. What do you have an overwhelming urge to do ... right now?

(Lights fade to blackout.)

THE END

A LOW-LYING FOG

by

John Yearley

The production of *A LOW-LYING FOG* at the Samuel French festival was directed by Erma Duricko. The Assistant Director was Karen Eterovich, and the original music and sound was by Jeff Duricko. The cast was:

PHIL   Trevor Jones
GREG   Jeff Pucillo

ABOUT THE AUTHOR

John Yearley is also the author of Eugene O'Neill Conference finalist *Bruno Hauptmann Kissed My Forehead*, *Ephemera* (winner of the John Gassner prize and third place in the Plays for the 21st Century Contest) and *Leap* (finalist for the Christopher Brian Wolk Award). He is also the author of the short plays *Hating Beckett, Moving Mom, Strangers Are Easy* and *All in Little Pieces*. He is a member of the Dramatists Guild and the Writers Guild of America East and is a MacDowell Fellow.

(Light comes up on two men, GREG and PHIL. GREG hears and responds to PHIL, but PHIL cannot hear GREG. They speak to the audience.)

PHIL. I don't see what good this is gonna do....
GREG. He needs to talk to somebody.
PHIL. I'm not disrespecting you ...
GREG. He's never been much of a talker....
PHIL. ... it's just that, things being what they are ...
GREG. I mean, he talks. Just not about things ...
PHIL. ... what could you say?
GREG. ... you know, things that matter.
PHIL. Really. I'm serious. What could you possibly say to me?
GREG. Just ... *talk.*

(Pause)

PHIL. Fine. *(Pause)* I was just trying to be a good brother....
GREG. He is a good brother,...
PHIL. I mean, it's the shit deal of the world, isn't it?
GREG. Yes, it is....
PHIL. I don't get it....
GREG. I'm so sorry....
PHIL. I mean, she just left!
GREG. Oh ... that.
PHIL. No explanation.
GREG. I thought he meant ....
PHIL. And he's like one of the best guys I ever met.
GREG. This is my little brother, you understand....
PHIL. And I'm not just saying that because he's my brother....
GREG. Yeah, right.
PHIL. I'm serious. Ask anyone....
GREG. He never saw my many blatant faults....
PHIL. My brother is a stand-up guy. He didn't deserve that shit.
GREG. Nobody deserves that shit.

PHIL. I mean, nobody deserves that shit.

GREG. Preach it, brother!

PHIL. But especially not him. Especially not him. *(Pause)* See, his wife, couple of months ago, she just fuckin' leaves him. Six years together. Happiest couple I ever saw.

GREG. I thought so.

PHIL. And then one day it's just, "I can't be married ..."

GREG. It wasn't quite that fast.

PHIL. "... I love you, but I can't be married...."

GREG. Felt that fast.

PHIL. "I'm sorry," she says.

GREG. She was, too. That's the amazing thing.

PHIL. "I'm sorry"? What the fuck is that supposed to mean?

GREG. Didn't mean much.

PHIL. So my brother, my fucking kick-ass brother ....

GREG. Not again ....

PHIL and GREG. *(Together.)* Best guy I ever met ....

PHIL. He's all alone. Everything he dreamed of ....

GREG. Gone.

PHIL. Home ....

GREG. Gone.

PHIL. Kids ...

GREG. Gone.

PHIL. He thought that they were going to grow old together....

GREG. I was wrong. On both counts.

PHIL. So he calls me. And he's a fucking wreck....

GREG. Couldn't even talk....

PHIL. He's making these noises, like an animal....

GREG. I could barely tell him what happened.

PHIL. So I tell him to get his ass up here. Right now.

GREG. I said "no," of course.

PHIL. He starts to say how he doesn't want to bother me ...

GREG. He wouldn't hear it....

PHIL. ... and I'm like, "Get your miserable ass up here RIGHT NOW...."

GREG. He's a good brother. Always has been....

PHIL. Bother me? I wanted to kick his ass for that.

GREG. So I drove up....

PHIL. He came right up....

GREG. Six hours later, I'm here. New Hampshire.

PHIL. I thought it would be good for him to get out of the city.

GREG. It's so beautiful up here.

PHIL. God, when I saw him ....

GREG. I lost it....

PHIL. I mean, he can barely stand. Walks over to me like a gimp, like a cripple....

GREG. It's like he's suffering for me....

PHIL. I've never seen him like that in my whole life....

GREG. You see that love, that empathy ....

PHIL. Broke my fuckin' heart....

GREG. Strips you naked.

PHIL. So he comes in and I give him a beer and we're talking ....

GREG. Not much to talk about....

PHIL. But it's a pretty short conversation ...

GREG. What do you say?

PHIL. ... because she's just gone! There's no reason. There's no problem to discuss.

GREG. Nothing to hash out....

PHIL. "I can't be married"?!

GREG. Pretty lame.

PHIL. What the hell are you supposed to do with that?

GREG. I'll never know.

PHIL. So I just sit there like an idiot. Telling him how sorry I am, how much I love him....

GREG. Tells me I don't deserve it. How I'm better off without her....

PHIL. I wanted to kill the fucking cunt.

GREG. "You don't want anything to do with a person who'd do something like that." That's what he said.

PHIL. I couldn't say anything. I was useless.

GREG. He was great.

(Pause)

PHIL. So, after sitting there with my thumb up my ass for awhile, I ask if he's hungry....

GREG. I'm not, of course....

PHIL. And he says "yes"....

GREG. I'd barely eaten in days....

PHIL. So I tell him about this great restaurant I know over in Manchester, right on the river.

GREG. I said it sounded great.

PHIL. So we go to my car. But, and this is the fucked-up thing, the thing I keep going over and over in my head ....

GREG. I wanted to sit in the back.

PHIL. He sits in the back seat! And I'm like, "Bro, what are you doing?"

GREG. I didn't want to talk.

PHIL. But he says he wants to sit in the back....

GREG. Couldn't talk.

PHIL. Says he just wants to stare out the window....

GREG. Couldn't look at him.

PHIL. So what am I gonna say? No? So I say, "fine."

GREG. I could tell he was upset....

PHIL. It bothered me, but what was I gonna do? So we go....

GREG. It was nice watching the scenery ...

PHIL. I didn't know whether or not he wanted to talk....

GREG. ... peaceful....

PHIL. I said a couple of things....

GREG. I pretended I couldn't hear him.

PHIL. But he couldn't hear me, so I stopped. Which was probably good because I couldn't see shit....

GREG. There was this fog, this low-lying fog blanketing everything....

PHIL. I haven't lived around here that long, so I have to pay attention or I'll get lost....

GREG. It was amazing.

PHIL. So we're driving for like ten minutes when, out of nowhere, up ahead, there's all these cars,...

GREG. It was strange, because we hadn't seen anybody up to that point....

PHIL. There's dozens of them, all parked along the side of the road....

GREG. I couldn't imagine what they were doing there.

PHIL. And I'm wondering what all those cars are doing there when I see that there's all this light coming through the fog up ahead. ...

GREG. Like a beacon....

PHIL. And when I get closer, I see this big tent. Like a circus tent....

GREG. This clean, amber light is pouring out of it....

PHIL. And there are all these people in suits and dresses, sitting at these fancy tables....

GREG. It was beautiful.

PHIL. And I think to myself, "Holy motherfucking shit!"...

GREG. A wedding....

PHIL. It's a wedding....

GREG. A big, beautiful wedding....

PHIL. And I feel like the asshole of the universe ...

GREG. How could he have known?

PHIL. ... I don't know what to do. So once I figure out what it is, I floor it. Haul his ass outta there!

GREG. Scared the shit out of me!

PHIL. No way he needs to see that.

GREG. But I did.

PHIL. Once we get past it, I look in the rear view mirror to check out how he's doing. And he was smiling....

GREG. I had to laugh.

PHIL. Can you believe that? He's got this wry little smile on his face.

GREG. Who says God doesn't have a sense of humor?

PHIL. And I'm just loving my brother so much. I mean, is he the most amazing guy in the world or what?

GREG. Just appreciating the joke.

(Pause)

PHIL. So, anyway, I keep driving. Only the thing is, I can't see shit.

GREG. The fog was so dense....

PHIL. I mean, my brights are reflecting off the fog, so I can't use them.

GREG. It's pitch black *and* foggy.

PHIL. So I take what I think is the right turn, but I can't really tell where I'm going....

GREG. And I, of course, have no idea.

PHIL. But I don't want him to worry, so I keep up a front....

GREG. But after a couple of minutes, I start to get this weird sense of *deja vu*.

PHIL. And I'm getting scared 'cause I think we're lost ...

GREG. Everything's looking weirdly familiar.

PHIL. ... when you know what I see up ahead?

GREG. Light.

PHIL. That light! Those cars!

GREG. I recognize it in a heartbeat.

PHIL. It's the wedding.

GREG. We went in a circle.

PHIL. It's the fucking wedding.

GREG. And this time there's no shock to dull the pain. I see everything....

PHIL. I can't believe it!

GREG. I see the bride, glowing....

PHIL. How could I do something like that?

GREG. I see the groom, dancing....

PHIL. Am I fucking retarded?

GREG. I see all of them. And they're so happy.

PHIL. So I floor it, just like before....

GREG. But it's too late. I'm gone....

PHIL. Once we get clear of it, I look in the mirror....

GREG. Sobs lurching out of my body like I'm puking....

PHIL. And he's losing it. Just losing it....

GREG. I didn't want to make him feel bad, so I try to stop....

PHIL. And I can see he's trying to hold back, so I just say to him, "Let it go, buddy...."

GREG. So I did. I let it all go.

PHIL. It wasn't pretty. I'll tell you that much. But he's my brother, so I don't care. *(Pause)* By the time we get to Manchester, he's quiet.

GREG. I'm horizontal is what I am.

PHIL. He's curled up in this little ball....

GREG. Can't even sit up.

PHIL. So I go back, open the door, and say, "We're here, bro ..."

GREG. "Just resting," I say.

PHIL. ... and he makes a fucking joke!

GREG. Trying to lessen the tension.

PHIL. Unbelievable. *(Pause)* So, we have dinner ...

GREG. The place is really nice....

PHIL. ... and it's all right, I guess....

GREG. Beautiful view of the river....

PHIL. But he doesn't say much. Barely touches his food.

GREG. I couldn't. I tried....

PHIL. He does say this one thing, though.

GREG. I did?

PHIL. Yeah, he's just sitting there, totally silent, when all of a sudden he says, "You know what she told me on my birthday? She told me that she was proud of me. She told me that she was proud of me every day."

GREG. Oh, yeah.

PHIL. And I didn't know what to say, so like an idiot I just go, "Yeah?"

GREG. I remember now.

PHIL. And he said, "Yeah. I wonder if she's proud of me now." And I didn't know what to say.

GREG. What could you say?

PHIL. So I didn't say anything. Maybe I should have. *(Pause)* Anyway, after only like forty-five minutes, we take off.

GREG. I go straight for the back.

PHIL. And he sits in the back seat. I don't say anything.

GREG. It was nice of him.

PHIL. So I'm driving back, and I'm really preoccupied, you know. About what he said, and trying to think of what I can do to help him....

GREG. And I'm just staring out the window ...

PHIL. So I don't even think about how I'm going back. Like the *route* I'm taking.

GREG. ... doing everything I can to hold myself together....

PHIL. I don't think about the one thing I can do. The one thing I should be keeping him from....

GREG. He makes it sound like it's his fault.

PHIL. I don't even see it until I'm right on top of it....

GREG. The light, the cars....

PHIL. 'Cause if I'd seen it, I'd have pulled right off the road....

GREG. I knew he wasn't paying attention.

PHIL. I'd have driven across somebody's lawn. I don't give a fuck.

GREG. He'd never do anything like that if he were paying attention.

PHIL. I'd have done something, *anything*....

GREG. But it was too late.

PHIL. But I was surrounded by cars on both sides.

GREG. It was like being in a tunnel.

PHIL. I couldn't pull over. And I couldn't speed up because this car was coming at us ...

GREG. That's when everything changed. I saw the headlights, and I felt like they were coming right at me.

PHIL. ... and it was coming so fast....

GREG. They looked so clean, knifing through the fog....

PHIL. I was worried it was going to hit us....

GREG. And all of a sudden it's the most obvious thing in the world.

PHIL. So I looked back at him to see how he was doing....

GREG. I couldn't believe I hadn't thought of it before....

PHIL. And this is the fucked-up thing. The thing I see when I close my eyes at night. He has, like, this little smile on his face ...

GREG. I know exactly what to do.

PHIL. ... like he was laughing at some private joke....

GREG. I felt an enormous burden lift from my shoulders....

PHIL. He looked *so happy*.

GREG. I looked over to the door. Unlocked.

PHIL. And I was so relieved, because I thought he would be flipping out.

GREG. All I'd have to do is pull up the handle and lean ....

PHIL. That's the thing I remember feeling. Before it happened.

GREG. Pull up and lean.

PHIL. ... That relief.

GREG. I was so relieved.

(A mechanical "Ding!" sound is heard.)

PHIL. But then I saw this light turn on on the dashboard ...

GREG. I lifted the handle ...

PHIL. It said, "Door ajar."

GREG. ... and I leaned.

(Pause)

PHIL. Tell you the truth, I don't remember much after that....

GREG. Me, either. It was pretty quick.

PHIL. Next thing I know, I'm standing over him....

GREG. I remember hitting the ground, seeing the wheels come at me....

PHIL. And he could be anybody, you know....

GREG. And then it ends. Blackout.

PHIL. Doesn't even look like my brother....

GREG. Ends for me, anyway. *(Pause. GREG turns to PHIL.)* I am so sorry, bro.

(Pause)

PHIL. So, that's it. That's the story.

GREG. More or less.

PHIL. So, now I want to ask you something. What do you think you're going to do for me? What little pearls of wisdom are you going to offer?

GREG. Don't be like that.

PHIL. You gonna tell me it's not my fault?

GREG. It isn't.

PHIL. You gonna tell me there was nothing I could have done?

GREG. There wasn't.

PHIL. Well, let me tell you something—I don't give a shit!

GREG. You have to stop.

(PHIL rises to leave.)

PHIL. I'm getting out of here.

GREG. Sit down....

PHIL. This is a waste of my fucking time....

GREG. Sit down....

PHIL. I don't even know why I came!

(PHIL is almost out the door when GREG screams at him.)

GREG. Sit down, goddammit! You sit your miserable ass in that chair RIGHT NOW! *(PHIL stops. He pauses at the door. He begins to cry.)* Good.... *(PHIL staggers back to the chair. He sits and weeps.)* Good....

PHIL. You wanna hear something crazy? Something totally whacked? Sometimes, when I'm quiet ... it's like I can hear him. Like he's talking to me....

(GREG breathes a tremendous sigh of relief. The lights slowly fade.)

THE END

SET

The set is simple, just a sofa or a couple of folding chairs.

COSTUME

Phil is dressed in jeans and a flannel shirt. Greg is slightly more professional, maybe slacks and a button-up shirt.

QUICK & DIRTY
(A Subway Fantasy)

by

David Riedy

QUICK & DIRTY (A Subway Fantasy) was developed through The Ensemble Studio Theatre's Lexington Lab (Curt Dempster, Artistic Director) under the direction of the author. MAN was first played by Jonathan Tipton Meyers, WOMAN was first played by Holli Harms.

QUICK & DIRTY (A Subway Fantasy) was subsequently produced by Tangent Theatre Company (Michael Rhodes and Keith Teller, Co-Artistic Directors; Andrea Miller Rhodes, Producing Director) as part of its *Subway Series* in June 2003 at the WorkShop Theater. The director was Greg Skura; lighting design by Deborah Constantine; original music by Aaron Hondros; sound design by Neil Miller; the production stage manager was Paul Molnar. The cast was as follows:

MAN	Michael Rhodes
WOMAN	Jill Van Note

ABOUT THE AUTHOR

David Riedy's work has been seen all over New York City, including: HERE, The Workshop Theatre, Manhattan Theatre Source, The Neighborhood Playhouse and The Ensemble Studio Theatre. His play *Late Night in the Women's Restroom of the Jungle Bar* was produced as part of E.S.T's 2001 Marathon of One Act Plays, and scenes from the play were included in *Best Stage Scenes of 2001*. As a founding member of The Lexington Group, David directed and was head writer of *The Ballad of Larry the Flyer*, which enjoyed runs at The 2001 Piccolo Spoleto Festival and the 2001 New York International Fringe Festival. He is also a head writer of *theAtrainplays* project with whom he has written nine short plays and musicals while riding the subway. He is a member of The Ensemble Studio Theatre and the Dramatists Guild.

CHARACTERS

WOMAN: wearing a silk blouse, opened one button below what would be considered "business-like," and a skirt. She is 31, with short, blonde hair, and a severe, sensual face.

MAN: 27, dark-skinned, with black hair and thick, black eyebrows. He is dressed in a ratty t-shirt with the name of some band he played bass for five years ago, over which is a faded dress shirt tucked into black jeans. He wears heavy black boots.

(Darkness. A barely understandable squawking voice announces a delay for all trains. Lights slowly fade up and reveal part of a New York subway platform. On one end stands a WOMAN, staring off left, waiting for the subway. She has a folded New York Times *in one hand, and a pencil held by her right ear. At her feet, a briefcase. At the other end of the platform, looking off right, is a MAN.*
They become aware of each other, and slowly turn to face one another. They lock eyes and stare, unabashedly, for a long, intense moment. The MAN walks with purpose over to the WOMAN.)

MAN. Do you want to go somewhere?

WOMAN. Excuse me?

MAN. Go somewhere we can be alone.

WOMAN. No thanks.

MAN. I noticed you looking at me.

WOMAN. Leave me alone.

MAN. I would, but you looked like you wanted to talk.

WOMAN. Do I know you?

MAN. No, but you smiled at me.

WOMAN. I don't smile at people I don't know.

MAN. There was something electric there.

WOMAN. I was looking at the paper.

MAN. Oh. Doing the crossword?

WOMAN. Yes.

MAN. I finished it this morning, if you want any help.

WOMAN. No thanks.

MAN. Okay. I don't like help either.

WOMAN. Thank you.

MAN. You weren't really doing the crossword.

WOMAN. Funny, I thought I was.

MAN. C'mon, admit it. You were looking at me.

WOMAN. What's a four-letter word for "an annoyance," starts with a "p" ...?

MAN. If you really want me to, I'll go.

WOMAN. … "pest."
MAN. I thought we connected.

(He turns, walks away.)

WOMAN. Why did you ask about the crossword?
MAN. The pencil in your ear.
WOMAN. Oh. Occupational hazard.
MAN. You're a pencil courier.
WOMAN. Editor.

(Beat.)

MAN. You were looking at me.
WOMAN. I was.
MAN. For a long time.
WOMAN. There's not much else to look at.
MAN. And you smiled at me.
WOMAN. I was remembering someone.
MAN. You were thinking something about me.
WOMAN. Look, I'm tired—
MAN. You were undressing me.
WOMAN. I don't think so.
MAN. You unzipped me with your eyes.
WOMAN. *(Looking.)* Still looks zipped.
MAN. You're playing with me.
WOMAN. This isn't playing. It's fending off.
MAN. We made eye contact and didn't look away. That never happens.
WOMAN. No, it doesn't.
MAN. There was something there.
WOMAN. I thought you were attractive. That's all.
MAN. Are you looking for someone?
WOMAN. No.
MAN. Should I believe that?
WOMAN. Every relationship is based on trust.
MAN. We have a relationship!
WOMAN. We're relating.
MAN. Oh. Semantics.

(A train approaches the station.)

WOMAN. The train. Thank god.

(She gets her things, and moves to the front of the platform, waiting for the train to stop.)

MAN. Do you know what I was thinking? While we were looking at each other?

WOMAN. I can guess.

MAN. "What if that lovely woman and I fell onto each other with our mouths open and eyes closed and had each other totally and without fear? It could be something sweet, something fun. What's wrong with tenderness?" *(The train comes to a stop and the doors open. During the following, she steps onto the subway and he puts his foot in front of the door, holding it open:)* The way you looked at me makes me think we could care about each other for a few hours which seems much better than dragging it out for months or years in a complicated ritual of trying to convince yourself that the momentary flash of lust or desire, or love—if you want to call it that—that that feeling can last past its natural lifetime of weeks or even seconds. That's the greatest sin two people can commit together. And I realized that there was nothing to stop us, me and you, or "us"—everyone— the whole world, there's no reason why two people can't be totally honest with each other and share feelings sparked by how someone said "peppercorn" or a smile, just a corner-smile, as they look bashfully down at their shoes, or the casual, unintended brush of someone's hand across your ass as they squeeze by in a doorway, or even the unlikely meeting of sympathetic and interested eyes from across a crowded subway platform.

(Beat. She exits the subway car. He removes his foot, the doors close and the subway leaves the station.)

WOMAN. You really mean all that?

MAN. Right now I do. Keep pushing me off and I won't much longer.

WOMAN. Why are you interested in me?

MAN. Didn't you just hear my speech? I thought I was being eloquent.

WOMAN. But me? Is it that I look like the kind of woman who would demurely blush and look away at a compliment?

MAN. No—

WOMAN. Is that the kind of woman you usually approach?

MAN. I've never done this before.

WOMAN. You seem to know all about casual connections.

MAN. I was speaking from my heart, off the top of my head.

WOMAN. Is that where you keep it?

MAN. What?

WOMAN. You talk a lot about vague feelings of attraction, but never specifics.

MAN. I'm telling you what I feel.

WOMAN. I want to know what it is about me that makes you want me.

MAN. It was this feeling—

WOMAN. Not feeling. Details.

MAN. I don't—?

WOMAN. What was it? My nipples becoming visible through my shirt as a breeze blew down from the street? My legs, and what they lead to? Were you thinking of burying your face between my thighs?

MAN. I—

WOMAN. You talk about making some kind of "connection" when all you really want is to get laid, isn't it?

MAN. No. That's not all.

WOMAN. You don't have to lie. There's nothing wrong with being hot.

MAN. It's not just sex. It's shedding all the baggage, avoiding the emotional black hole that goes with being with someone, and sharing this moment.

WOMAN. Want to know what I was thinking, while we were exchanging looks?

MAN. Please.

(Beat.)

WOMAN. I came down the stairs from the street, and nearly fell. I slipped on the front of a step, in a hurry because I didn't want to miss the train. I wanted to be home in my bathrobe, on the couch, drinking CranApple juice and doing the crossword. That's all I've thought about all day at work: "CranApple and crossword." There's no train. Instead, there's an announcement; a delay. I drop my briefcase and fall against the wall, worn out. More and more people arrive, stand, lean against the wall. I watch, eyes half-closed, unamused. But then, an interesting man. Somewhat attractive. Black jeans, heavy boots—to be stylish, he doesn't do construction, that's obvious—he's an intellectual, or thinks he is. But he is attractive. His face has large, inviting, sensual features. Big, soft lips, a substantial nose. And his eyebrows intrigue me. They're very dark and thick, and lifted to an almost unbelievably cocky height. I imagine those eyebrows, pushed down in concentration, his whole face intent, as this man lays underneath me and carefully inserts his large—generously large—erect penis inside of me. I'm sitting back on my feet, balancing on the couch, my bathrobe untied and wide-open. A glass of CranApple and a yellow No. 2 pencil in my left hand. I take a gulp while you carefully maneuver your pelvis to rub nice and slow, and I look at my other hand, with the crossword in it, and 18-across is a nine-letter word ending with "n." The clue is "the king was one," and as I look down at your sexy, bush eyebrows to tell you in a voice made deep by your "attentions" that the answer is "swordsman" ... you walk up and interrupt me.

(Simmer. Simmer.)

MAN. Come home with me.
WOMAN. No.
MAN. Somewhere, anywhere—
WOMAN. I'm not going anywhere with you.
MAN. After—that—you won't—?
WOMAN. What for?
MAN. To consummate our—this—this "relationship"—it's not even a relationship—this new thing that we're creating, this momentary moment of understanding and love.
WOMAN. You truly believe that, don't you?
MAN. I want to give myself to you, completely.
WOMAN. For an hour.
MAN. For however long.
WOMAN. Which you'll decide.
MAN. We'll decide.
WOMAN. This is all about control.
MAN. No, it's not.
WOMAN. You want it all on your terms.
MAN. Don't make this into some kind of political, gender thing.
WOMAN. You want to have this— *(mocking:) this*—for as long as it suits you. For as long as it's fun. And easy.

MAN. Now you've ruined it.

WOMAN. As soon as it got complicated, involved actual emotions instead of hormonal responses, you'd be gone.

MAN. It could have been—nice.

WOMAN. Fuck nice. I don't want nice. I want steaming hot slippery sex—

MAN. Yes.

WOMAN. —with someone, anyone, who can look me in the eye afterward and tell me exactly what they feel and believe in and want and who cares for me with a mixture of love and need and anger and sweet sweet tenderness that I could possibly never untangle. And you couldn't be that for me.

MAN. Why not?

WOMAN. But you're good enough to think about with your clothes off, so I thought about it. And I liked it.

MAN. You're afraid.

WOMAN. Of what?

MAN. Of someone living up to your fantasy.

WOMAN. I was very generous in my imagination.

MAN. What do you want? What do you want? Do you really want someone to hold you after you come, while you become heavy and drowsy in his arms? Or are you just looking for the fucking of a lifetime?

WOMAN. I fucked you already. You were good. I'll give you a cigarette if you want.

MAN. What would have happened, after the sex?

WOMAN. Why do you insist on taking this further than what it is?

MAN. You used me.

WOMAN. You did the same thing to me.

MAN. I wanted more than sex.

WOMAN. You wanted emotional control.

MAN. I wanted to share something with you.

WOMAN. To give me a gift.

MAN. As equals.

WOMAN. On your terms.

MAN. Maybe I was wrong. Maybe it's impossible for two people to ever truly share anything. Maybe we're better off not trying. Maybe I should resign myself to selfish gratification, like you. *(Beat.)* And yes—I would love to lick your thighs and nibble your nipples.

WOMAN. In your dreams.

MAN. And yours.
WOMAN. No. You dream. I fantasize.
MAN. There's a difference?
WOMAN. I don't fool myself that what I imagine is real. *(Beat. They stare at each other.)* I'm taking a cab.

(She exits. He watches all the way down the platform, until she's out of sight, then turns and stares off, down the tracks, as lights fade to black.)

THE END

PROPERTY LIST

The New York Times (WOMAN)
Pencil (WOMAN)
Briefcase WOMAN)

ABOUT THE SET

Set should be minimal. A sign with a subway stop's street name, or "After-hour trains stop here" is enough to create location. The subway can be suggested with sound and lighting up part of the stage on its arrival, and dimming on its departure.

THE FERRY

by

Ryan Hill

THE FERRY was written for and originally produced by Melissa Rayworth in October, 2001, as part of Big City, Short Plays—A Benefit Evening for Windows on Hope.

THE FERRY was performed as part of Vital Signs New Works Festival at Vital Theatre Company (Artistic Director: Stephen Sunderlin and Managing Director: Sharon Fallon) in May, 2002. It was directed by Karen Sommers with:

MAN	Adam Groves
WOMAN	Dawn Scanlan

ABOUT THE AUTHOR

Born and raised in northern Wisconsin, Ryan Hill has lived in Berlin and New York and currently resides in Minneapolis. Also a performer and director, he is a Fulbright Scholar and has worked with seminal director Robert Wilson.

PRODUCTION NOTE

The physical design elements of *THE FERRY* are few. It is highly recommended to keep necessary props, costumes and sets simple and complimentary to the clean style of the piece.

(A WOMAN stands outside on the Staten Island Ferry. A MAN approaches her.)

MAN. Hey.
WOMAN. Hey.
MAN. —
WOMAN. —
MAN. —
WOMAN. —
MAN. So.
WOMAN. So.
MAN. You going to Staten Island?
WOMAN. Yeah.
MAN. —
WOMAN. —
MAN. You ever been to Staten Island?
WOMAN. Yes.
MAN. You live there?
WOMAN. No.
MAN. Oh.
WOMAN. —
MAN. —
WOMAN. —
MAN. I live in Staten Island.
WOMAN. —
MAN. —
WOMAN. —
MAN. I wouldn't lie about a thing like that.
WOMAN. No?
MAN. Never.
WOMAN. —
MAN. I'm proud of it.
WOMAN. Oh.
MAN. You from Staten Island?
WOMAN. No.

MAN. But you've been there.

WOMAN. Yes.

MAN. And that's where you're going.

WOMAN. Unless this ferry's going to Hoboken.

MAN. No. This ferry's going to Staten Island.

WOMAN. I know.

MAN. This here's the world famous Staten Island ferry. You heard of it?

WOMAN. I'm on it.

MAN. Did you want to go to Hoboken?

WOMAN. No.

MAN. Oh.

WOMAN. —

MAN. You ever been to Hoboken?

WOMAN. Yes.

MAN. —

WOMAN. —

MAN. I've never been to Hoboken.

WOMAN. —

MAN. —

WOMAN. —

MAN. You from Staten Island?

WOMAN. I already told you—

MAN. 'Cause I'm from Staten Island.

WOMAN. No, I'm not from Staten Island.

MAN. You work in Staten Island?

WOMAN. No.

MAN. Where you from?

WOMAN. I'm from Iowa.

MAN. —

WOMAN. —

MAN. —

WOMAN. —

MAN. Isn't that in Suffolk County?

WOMAN. No.

MAN. Oh. I ain't never been there. Where do you live, if you don't live in Staten Island?

WOMAN. I live in Manhattan.

MAN. Oh.

WOMAN. You ever been there?

MAN. No.

WOMAN. —

MAN. —

WOMAN. —

MAN. Is that in Suffolk County?

WOMAN. You're serious?

MAN. —

WOMAN. You don't know what Manhattan is?

MAN. I ain't no worldly guy. I'm just a simple guy from—

BOTH. Staten Island.

WOMAN. I know. Where did you get on this ferry?

MAN. Staten Island.

WOMAN. No, I mean just now, before we left the dock.

MAN. Staten Island.

WOMAN. No, just a couple minutes ago, you got on the ferry, right?

MAN. No.

WOMAN. What do you mean, "no"? You're standing here, aren't you?

MAN. Yeah.

WOMAN. Then you got on the ferry in Manhattan.

MAN. No. I got on the ferry in Staten Island.

WOMAN. Wait a minute, you just rode the ferry from Staten Island to Manhattan and now you're riding it back?

MAN. Back from where?

WOMAN. Look behind you.

MAN. Why?

WOMAN. That's Manhattan.

MAN. Where?

WOMAN. See all those buildings? See that island?

MAN. Yeah.

WOMAN. That's Manhattan.

MAN. Oh.

WOMAN. So this ferry runs between Manhattan and Staten Island.

MAN. No.

WOMAN. 'No' what?

MAN. This ferry runs between Staten Island and Staten Island.

WOMAN. But it stops between trips. It crosses the water and goes to Manhattan, then goes back to Staten Island.

MAN. Oh, yeah. It does, but it's not important.

WOMAN. Didn't you wonder why the boat stopped and everyone got off?

MAN. No.

WOMAN. Didn't you think that was strange to do if it hadn't stopped somewhere important?

MAN. No.

WOMAN. Why?

MAN. 'Cause it does that all day.

WOMAN. Do you ride this thing all day?

MAN. No.

WOMAN. —

MAN. I go home at night.

WOMAN. So you ride the Staten Island ferry all day.

MAN. No. I get up in the morning, then get on the ferry.

WOMAN. And you've never gotten off in Manhattan?

MAN. Listen, lady. I'm sorry, but you're not making much sense. The ferry goes in one direction. It goes from Staten Island to Staten Island. Anything in between doesn't matter.

WOMAN. What do you think's going on behind you? In all those buildings? What do you think's happening back there?

MAN. Doesn't matter.

WOMAN. That's the heart and soul of this country, the machinery that makes the world go around is back there. Can't you feel the energy?

MAN. Doesn't matter.

WOMAN. How can you say that?

MAN. Because it doesn't matter.

WOMAN. Those towers, all those people.... All the sweat and tears it took to build this country is condensed right there. That is the island of infinite possibilities. People from every corner of this planet come to this skyline because they know hard work and talent will pay off. They know anything is possible. How can you say it doesn't matter? Look at it. That's progress, the city of dreams.

MAN. You want to talk about forward, but you keep looking backwards.

WOMAN. Fine. What's forward to you?

MAN. That's forward.

WOMAN. And what's that?

BOTH. Staten Island.

WOMAN. —

MAN. —

WOMAN. You know what that is?

MAN. Statue of Liberty.

WOMAN. And you don't know what Manhattan is?

MAN. —

WOMAN. Wait a minute, how do you know where Suffolk County is?

MAN. That's where my mom grew up.

WOMAN. You've never been there?

MAN. No.

WOMAN. Don't you have any relatives or anything back there? Grandparents you visited?

MAN. Nope.

WOMAN. Why not?

MAN. They all live in Staten Island now.

WOMAN. —

MAN. You hungry?

WOMAN. No.

MAN. 'Cause I'm gonna have dinner.

WOMAN. You bring food with you?

MAN. Don't you?

WOMAN. What do you have in there?

MAN. Some grapes. Chicken. Ham sandwich.

WOMAN. Where did you get that stuff?

MAN. Staten—

WOMAN. I mean what store?

MAN. The grocery store.

WOMAN. Do you have a job?

MAN. What do you mean?

WOMAN. Where did you get the money to buy that food?

MAN. What do you mean?

WOMAN. You bought that food, right?

MAN. —

WOMAN. Did you steal that?

MAN. What do you mean?

WOMAN. Jesus, you stole all that? You're a thief.

MAN. Listen, lady. I don't know where you're from, but things are different out here on Staten Island.

WOMAN. Not that different.

MAN. How would you know? Are you from Staten Island?

WOMAN. No.

MAN. Then don't criticize our ways of doing things.

WOMAN. Stealing isn't legal no matter where it is.

MAN. Call it what you want. I've got food.

WOMAN. So do I, but I didn't steal it.

MAN. You've got food?

WOMAN. Yes.

MAN. Show me.

WOMAN. *(She pulls out a candy bar.)* And I didn't steal it.

MAN. Good for you.

WOMAN. —

MAN. —

WOMAN. What's that over there?

MAN. I don't know.

WOMAN. It's Brooklyn.

MAN. Whatever.

WOMAN. You've never heard of Brooklyn?

MAN. Maybe.

WOMAN. What about that, you know what that is?

MAN. A park.

WOMAN. Do you know what the city's called?

MAN. No

WOMAN. That's Jersey City. And all of that is New Jersey.

MAN. Sure.

WOMAN. And back over there is Newark. And further up the river is the Bronx. And further up the other river is Queens. And past New Jersey is Pennsylvania, that way is Philadelphia, Pittsburgh's that way. Massachusetts and Boston are up that way, by Connecticut, Rhode Island, Vermont, New Hampshire, Maine, upstate New York— you have heard of New York, right?

MAN. *(Shrugs while eating.)*

WOMAN. This is ludicrous. You've never heard of Washington, D.C.? Our capital? Baltimore? Maryland? Virginia? You ever heard of Florida? Do you know Disneyland?

MAN. Something about a big mouse, right?

WOMAN. What about … Chicago? Minnesota? Denver? New Mexico? Mexico? California? Have you ever heard of Los Angeles? Do you know what Hollywood is?

MAN. It's a big wooden sign.

WOMAN. Well … yes … but that's a part of a city called Los Angeles.

MAN. So?

WOMAN. So? So, it's important to know these things.

MAN. Why?

WOMAN. It gives us a sense of where we are.

MAN. I know where I am.

WOMAN. Yeah, you're on the ferry. But don't you want to know where other people are from?

MAN. I know where you're from, you told me. You're from someplace near Suffolk County.

WOMAN. Iowa is not near Suffolk County.

MAN. Oh. Then where is it?

WOMAN. See? See what I mean? If you knew what these places were, you'd be able to identify people.

MAN. Identify them how?

WOMAN. Well, you'd be able to know that I'm from Iowa. And you'd know what that means.

MAN. What does that mean?

WOMAN. I mean to say that, you'd be able to know me better.

MAN. How's that?

WOMAN. Well, you'd know what people are like there.

MAN. What's it like in Iowa?

WOMAN. Well, Iowa's in the Midwest. There's lots of rural areas. Lots of farms. It's not real progressive. There's a lot of corn. People don't think Iowans are very smart. Um ... I don't know.

MAN. So if I knew what Iowa was, and you told me you were from Iowa, then I'd know right away that you're a farmer, you're not very progressive, you're not very smart and you eat corn.

WOMAN. That's not what I meant.

MAN. Do you like corn?

WOMAN. That's not the point.

MAN. Are you progressive?

WOMAN. I'd like to think so.

MAN. Are you a farmer?

WOMAN. No.

MAN. Then, since you're none of those things, and I know you're smart, what good does it do me to know where Iowa is?

WOMAN. Okay. Okay, so that's not a good example. But what if you meet someone from another country. It would help to know where they're from.

MAN. What other country?

WOMAN. Say a man from Japan came up to you. If you knew he was from Japan, you'd know that –

MAN. He liked corn?

WOMAN. No.

MAN. He doesn't like corn?

WOMAN. No, that's not the point.

MAN. What does he eat?

WOMAN. I don't know … sushi and rice and dumplings and things.

MAN. So I'd know that. What else would I know.

WOMAN. You'd know you have to treat him different.

MAN. Why?

WOMAN. Well, because he's from Japan.

MAN. Why would I treat him differently?

WOMAN. Because … well … he's not from here.

MAN. You're not from Staten Island and I treat you like you're from Staten Island.

WOMAN. Alright. That's not my point.

MAN. I'm sorry, lady, but I've missed your point.

WOMAN. My point is that if you know where someone is from, you automatically know some things about them that can help you act differently towards them.

MAN. —

WOMAN. —

MAN. Okay.

WOMAN. See?

MAN. Why would I want to treat people differently?

WOMAN. —

MAN. —

WOMAN. Because people are different.

MAN. But they're all still people.

WOMAN. Sure, but … not everyone's from Staten Island.

MAN. I know that.

WOMAN. —

MAN. So, how should I treat you?

WOMAN. Like normal.

MAN. What's normal?

WOMAN. —

MAN. —

WOMAN. Like I'm from Staten Island.

(The man smiles.)

MAN. Want a grape?

(Blackout.)

THE END

OFF-OFF-BROADWAY
FESTIVAL PLAYS

THIRTEENTH SERIES
Beached   A Grave Encounter   No Problem   Reservations for Two
Strawberry Preserves   What's a Girl to Do

FOURTEENTH SERIES
A Blind Date with Mary   Bums   Civilization and Its Malcontents   Do Over
Tradition 1A

FIFTEENTH SERIES
The Adventures of Captain Neato-Man   A Chance Meeting Chateau Rene
Does This Woman Have a Name?   For Anne   The Heartbreak Tour
The Pledge

SIXTEENTH SERIES
As Angels Watch   Autumn Leaves   Goods   King of the Pekinese Yellowtail
Uranium   Way Deep   The Whole Truth   The Winning Number

SEVENTEENTH SERIES
Correct Address   Cowboys, Indians and Waitresses   Homebound   The Road
to Nineveh   Your Life Is a Feature Film

EIGHTEENTH SERIES
How Many to Tango?   Just Thinking   Last Exit Before Toll   Pasquini the
Magnificent   Peace in Our Time   The Power and the Glory
Something Rotten in Denmark   Visiting Oliver

NINETEENTH SERIES
Awkward Silence   Cherry Blend with Vanilla   Family Names   Highwire
Nothing in Common   Pizza: A Love Story   The Spelling Bee

TWENTIETH SERIES
Pavane   The Art of Dating   Snow Stars   Life Comes to the Old Maid   The
Appointment   A Winter Reunion

TWENTY-FIRST SERIES
Whoppers   Dolorosa Sanchez   At Land's End   In with Alma
With or Without You   Murmurs   Ballycastle

TWENTY-SECOND SERIES
Brothers   This Is How It Is   Because I Wanted to Say Tremulous   The Last
Dance   For Tiger Lilies Out of Season   The Most Perfect Day

OFF-OFF-BROADWAY
FESTIVAL PLAYS

TWENTY-THIRD SERIES
The Way to Miami   Harriet Tubman Visits a Therapist   Meridan, Mississippi
Studio Portrait   It's Okay, Honey   Francis Brick Needs No Introduction

TWENTY-FOURTH SERIES
The Last Cigarette   Flight of Fancy   Physical Therapy   Nothing in the World Like It
The Price You Pay   Pearls Ophelia   A Significant Betrayal

TWENTY-FIFTH SERIES
Strawberry Fields   Sin Inch Adjustable   Evening Education   Hot Rot
A Pink Cadillac Nightmare   East of the Sun and West of the Moon

TWENTY-SIXTH SERIES
Tickets, Please!   Someplace Warm   The Test   A Closer Look
A Peace Replaced   Three Tables

TWENTY-SEVENTH SERIES
Born to Be Blue   The Parrot   Flights   A Doctor's Visit
Three Questions   The Devil's Parole

TWENTY-EIGHTH SERIES
Along for the Ride   A Low-Lying Fog   Blueberry Waltz   The Ferry
Leaving Tangier   Quick & Dirty (A Subway Fantasy)

TWENTY-NINTH SERIES
All in Little Pieces   The Casseroles of Far Rockaway   Feet of Clay
The King and the Condemned   My Wife's Coat   The Theodore Roosevelt Rotunda

THIRTIETH SERIES
Defacing Michael Jackson   The Ex   Kerry and Angie   Outside the Box
Picture Perfect   The Sweet Room

THIRTY-FIRST SERIES
Le Supermarché   Libretto   Play #3   Sick   Pischer   Relationtrip

THIRTY-SECOND SERIES
Opening   Circuit Breakers   Bright. Apple. Crush.
The Roosevelt Cousins, Thoroughly Sauced   Every Man   The Good Book

THIRTY-THIRD SERIES
F*cking Art   Ayravana Flies *or* A Pretty Dish   The Thread Men
The Dying Breed   The Grave   Juniper; Jubilee

THIRTY-FOURTH SERIES
Drop   The Education of Macoloco   realer than that
The Student   Thucydides   Just Knots

SAMUELFRENCH.COM